CIEN SONETOS

Iván Argüelles

Francesco Petrarca, 1304 – 1375

With a Foreword by Jack Foley

And an Afterword by John M. Bennett

2019
Luna Bisonte Prods

CIEN SONETOS
© Iván Argüelles 2018

"Todo lo que somos es memoria
cuando creemos ser nostoros mismos."

- Miguel Angel Asturias, *Leyendas de Guatemala*

Cover art and book design by C. Mehrl Bennett
Back cover photo of Iván Argüelles by Raymond Holbert

The image reproduced on the title page is in the public domain and was also used as source material for the front cover. It is a portrait of Francesco Petrarca, July 20 1304 – July 18 1374. Petrarca was a famous Italian philosopher, scholar, and poet who was deemed the "father of Renaissance humanism". These sonnets use the Petrarchan sonnet form.

LBP

ISBN 978-1-938521-51-5

https://www.lulu.com/lunabisonteprods

LUNA BISONTE PRODS
137 Leland Ave.
Columbus, OH 43214 USA

FOR IVÁN ARGÜELLES UPON HIS COMPLETION
OF ONE HUNDRED SONNETS

> "none is greater than the breath
> that lingers above the mouth a year and many more a soul
> linked to nothing but its other in name only a s*ound*"

A *little* sound, a sonnet
One hundred sonnets sitting on a wall
One hundred sonnets ready to take on the entire Petrarchan tradition
Four lines four lines three lines three lines

Argüelles is like Petrarch like Sydney like Spenser like Shakespeare like Berryman
Like thousands of others taking on the son-Net
(David Bromige made a poem about his child and, though it was not fourteen lines,
Called it a son-net)

Congrats on the C note to the Bard of la calle Walnut
He has survived deaths in his time
He has made a great moan out of music

He has looked Death in the face and told it,
Thou art nothing but the great Enigma, Oblivion
I have long sought thee in my soul, and I care naught what thou dost.

Thou, dust.

Jack Foley   6/09/2018

SONNET #1   (June 1, 2018)

can the confines of one's life so contract
as narrows then fail to notice shrinking
the light the very shapes shadows no longer
make attributes of a still lesser hour declining

against rock or the leavening water below
in the dank kingdom promised to one and all
with its blank princess she of the dark pool
the unreflecting where no face stares back

no flower its petals recalls no lamp shines
a childhood missed in the turning leaves
a cosmos no larger than the passing waist

of sand in its tribulation to accumulate time
just so this minute twice brighter then fast
fades the relinquished hand no longer holds

SONNET #2   (June 2, 2018)

so what of the dreams our cameras followed
deep into night's unbuilt architecture under
scored sounding waves the waters lessened
by light's absence the towers to the left of space

reunion with myth and tapestry devolving
darkness around the swift of hair the swept
behind worlds of dusk a single and final once
word a signal flashing in hidden decibels

each a hand of music a beautiful echoing
but never to be heard again nor the x-ray
nor the fabulous of statues the speech aloud

only whispers in the sadly lost like a section
of air painted the color of oblivion a margin
leaves and otherwise silence the invisible

SONNET #3   (June 2, 2018)

I am become something more than myself
a dissolution of air the unimaginable a music
unheard by the composer initiating chords
to be struck in sleep long after death has

impossibilities of being myself the beyond
outside memory writing as only zephyrus can
words unraveling between leaf and branch
the shape of Primavera her gossamer skin

the light radiating from within the unspoken
syntax of statues again becoming other than
fleet of foot Diana of the imagination spurned

go then from the fetters of thought into sublime
up there can reach with unfeeling hands at
last the inarticulate by you I have become

SONNET #4   (June 02, 2018)

the world that beautiful in the blink of an eye
caught then dispersed in reds the shadows
behind sight fleeting against dark the coming
before day's end the memory and thought

of rock and light things brought together for
a moment drawn on the shutter and brought down
night that is wrapped around the tombstone
a recollection carved in some archaic sound

will we too then pass through ears of sand
stars and moon and comets fiery bright bereft
like statuary dissolved into the common ground

strained through a sieve of gods inchoate myth
ranunculus and butterfly thin streams of wind
rushing consonants scattered suns eternity undone

SONNET #5   (June 3, 2018)

at your approach night's dark hand shaping
ink of dreams softness billowing afterthought
footprints in air disheveled leaves a storm
whatever the mind undoes in a moment's hour

come back should you ever stair-top distance
wrapped incognito sibylline counterfeit sleep
the sheep in the eyes writing echo's monument
and falling you detach shadow from frame

so too water issues from stone honey from brick
words never uttered your bosom stain a frail
the fade of your gone tomorrows a wing stained

not return questions some grass a script of sand
none can read the remotely thumbed pages torn
from the indistinct passage of your pale longing

SONNET #6   (June 3, 2018)

nor does anchored to clouds sleep resolve a
day's fitful going through and fingers a thought
shaking quietly in midstream summers long
pale the image of revolving narcissus bloomed

only to drown mirror face down in what were
tempests of ink shadowing so remotely the
inveterate footfalls of the gone before illumined
in brief skirts of time their wrists expunged

of pulse the radios only in the head alert to songs
who can ever recall what they sang so far away
islands of shattered vistas a water elevated high

in atmospheres once Olympian divine domain
never attained nor in mind ever circling the heat
now diminished the petals wither and fade away

SONNET #7 (June 3, 2018)

so much and so little to do the years remaining
ancient and small their vicissitudes dolorous
content of sealed envelopes secretly like you
dreamt or perhaps never been but in footnotes

a shape or built on sand a house darker than
before when only the painted lilies seemed to
breathe tropic essences jade beside a floating
wall how could the beyond be so terribly near

charted fevers illustrated zeroes lengthening
and cryptic silhouettes drawn across afternoons
lacking skies and the homophones of light

we are come to this dark place this folded hill
buried its treasured being like a face traced
forever in precious but evanescent dewfall

SONNET #8   (June 3, 2018)

language isn't this a violent tenderness
shoes not returned shoulders emotions a
distance never to be why shouldn't it speak
to us as through statues of grass and wind

cannot come to terms with love nor ink a
space somewhere to the side of the mountain
with wings that night flies puzzled at so many
lights pinpricks of consciousness so far gone

a soliloquy of stone the cliff-side roaring
silently surf and white-caps dunning the sky
that trembling mirage of a single summer past

not question the syllables the rushing issue
of oracular sounds underneath where a soul
the body quizzes passing a fantasy of light

SONNET #9   (June 3, 2018)

vast a dawn threaded through its red aperture
horses painted the color of Nemesis rushing
waters at breakneck speed for a moment only
subsides again the broken memory of them

listening still for the dusky hooves to strike
or cloud breaks bursting to stem the immensity
of all that has never been but in a thimble
of light disbelief of flowers and pearly dew

now comes day the unborn its attributes of
tree rock stem lamentation and brief breathing
latter the sainted grief of unremembered echoes

the number of them the transient color of pale
fraught with unsuspecting hours sand itself
capsized in the small beautiful pool of oblivion

SONNET #10   (June 3, 2018)

passion wasn't to neglect but to fourfold
ecstasy a Sicilian brow pearled with arcana
sweat of the hour painted black like the horses
of the sun stunned banners flying wildly

just so we were returned unopened breaths
a continent of lost futures who could say why
the coffin was so small the letters so faded
another day will never come to echo this one

believe me tears sustained voluble the night
which is speaking through veins inarticulate
we will never understand the what of sadness

dank underside of sleep the queen in her porphyry
offers no shadow no delight of endless time
nothing but the broken syllable of her flower

SONNET #11   (June 3, 2018)

quick green the spill or are they irises
shedding summers of light to breathe
tell him but won't wake again this month
so moons have passed as well the drought

of a simple hour without color shadows
moving like walls against the fertility of
absence it's so swift the body then ashes
pronouns become useless and their sounds

a mask a person a stain of grass a vision a
tripartite version of sky blossoming at once
underneath the eye no longer sees does it

shaking the will off its tomb and caresses it
longing for marble the cold luster at night
when booming roots the cadaver to its echo

SONNET #12 (June 3, 2018)

are a bone and its text the smothering air
configurations of mind or dotted absences
moon craters devouring the light remaining
of this life our earthly presences distilled

I saw you once unraveling your shadow against
the pale thought you were having like water rushing
through stone afternoons at a time until the hill
behind it opaque myths the size of conjectures

we will never know if it dries the words around it
a sea of sandy reflections in the darkening oval
you seized like a glove the passing wind to fit

nor can we ever read what's below the page
grass leaves sectioned skies of murmuring
childhoods spent in the instant of becoming

SONNET #13   (June 4, 2018)

cryptic isn't it what a distance can make
silences too the well-springs of mind the
total unreflecting self pinned to its night
oncoming specters shaking wings of dust

to ever wake to weeks of astonishing light
like water appearing at the window breaking
one at a time the minutes into days of
grieving and watch the mirrors passing

into the month when dark folds its skirts
like moths yearning to burn in texts of flame
lamented and inscrutable smoke of destiny

reaping words fields of sound oracular remote
of stone birthing space and the tumult
blind hands reaching out for dusk dissolving

SONNET #14   (June 4, 2018)

here I offer you this bouquet of glass bees
parched humming of dehiscent earth its reds
opening like swarms of light iridescent high
in the opaline absence of gone heavens

you ask nothing more fingers of dust quivering
in an interlinear text between languages
of forged inks and the sand that resolves
etymologies more archaic than stone or air

reading it beneath gravity and the unknown
origins of stars in the wake of sleeping until
the old deliquescent syllables seem to echo

loud in the stifled ear of water the unseen
undoing myths far below dark consciousness
the littered orthography of unread mysteries

SONNET #15   (June 4, 2018)

to the dead myriad alephs in husks of light
of recent memory or of no recollection at
all a poetry of distances or quires dizzying
like insects the puzzle of a fleeting mind

yours too bitterly quiescent on a sloping street
criss-crossing like dragonflies over a water
darkened by the hill of time or pyramids such
as shadows construct come eventide alone

abandoned to thoughts I am of the many gone
in their suits and ties blouses and pinafores
heroic and sad in their starched pose of fate

which of the countless the one did I most love
and to lose fading that critical day of stucco walls
absence more precious than the vanished sun

SONNET #16   (June 4, 2018)

wounded without being wounded the heart
cornfield in the sun blazing afternoons far
from the nearest pool in a long white absence
this one line tossed threading narrow shadows

separating what converges from what disappears
confirming darkness which you pale thinking
other what had not been written using an ink
blown issuing from the sky's unseen origin

aches the drumming cloud extending a shadow
of light remote a beam entering mind's eye a
frame full of fists inchoate deepening earths

is spent the spear flying from an invisible hand
to a zone of blank ciphers spreading imitations
of leaves life falling against walls long undone

SONNET #17   (June 4, 2018)

rainbow with a hundred feet drinking profound
abyss wasn't it you were on the opposite bank
a boat flower-laden from the past phantomatic
without beginning but doomed an omega to end

shaking trees wild shadows lifted into a paradise
no more than inches from the parallel of your
self becoming less than that sudden bolt entering
the remote theater where puzzled we joined hands

lighting mysteriously the moving screen above
star after star erased from its name eerie vegetation
of humans learning to undress their speech of sleep

statuary blessing unformed nature hush blowing
greenery across the motionless sky a radiance left
to itself to die a painting on a momentary shade

SONNET #18   (June 4, 2018)

brother ? what brother love was I talking to
cinemascope version of day telling its twilight
the hour is up the whole diminished by its half
a reality that night curtains with bright cyanide

if his hemisphere were a speech act a symbol
syntax of grapheme and hand-shake louder
than recalled sitting there on the stone calling
art the life we should have been from the start

collapsed etymons a reefer on the side grass
what they refer to as adolescent euphoria parade
strutting big in a cloud tarnished by light

itself the shadow music of a stoned silhouette
singing sweet into the leaf a paranormal vision
brother the subscript on the dark side of infinity

SONNET #19   (June 4, 2018)

if you don't pay attention to language then
what's bitter is more so and sweet longing
for death the kisses imprinted on masks
fading from sight equidistant from the light

itself the inarticulate and fabulous to the
memory of what senses can contain all
moments being final all breath but done
in that instantaneous chiaroscuro snapshot

so speak no more or perhaps question why
these grasses so soon to wither these leaves
so arcane about to fall a dark presentiment

can no more be summoned back to life
is that a reason to close the choir and don
weeds bitterly intransigent this pale body

SONNET #20   (June 4, 2018)

stuttering and what else comes to ear
hearing the most distant star still unborn
before you died ephemeral photograph
of sound waves rippling through dusk

eternal *the* and all the other articles of
faith redundant assembled on the edge of
time the restless sky the inadmissible space
shifting a mass of red opaque thunderheads

across the summer waters and flying things
opalescent invertebrate constructs of mind
you can almost see listening to that crash !

booming *the* and swiftly inchoate and longing
you are unborn as that remote star that asterisk
in the spanish pandemonium of the dying light

SONNET #21   (June 4, 2018)

then what am I to say about the self dark
matter transpired dispersed neurons activated
pulse plasm and despair the light unfortunate
invading cellular depths don't come back !

to say the least damnation coruscating stellar
ceilings unobtainable the gods a laughing host
circulating nerve streams short circuited summer
even so tender it seems a thought reveries long

about the soul too its counterpart photons glyphs
disjunct poetries or thrombosis a brain in name
only a seeing to the other side of the eye a lexicon

invertebrate syllables how much can be retained a
hand or its other or three hemispheres combined
a cathedral the night a sighing before all silence

SONNET #22   (June 4, 2018)

and what doesn't matter and what if it rotates
and the words don't come out right a confession
of light a fugue an anticipation of finally the dark
at the end of the street just before lamps were

invented or heat distributed in cycles to lovers
hidden their depths of skin a story told out loud
be quiet or so it seemed a scent in the gloaming
of perfumes and opium the thunderous ending

who would have suspected from stairways and wells
the way life is a corner only and the distinct inversion
of walls just to the beside of the trees lining night

so come out Soul become the insubstantial you
were meant to be a hive of yellowing otherness
myself the you a pronoun in distress a longing

SONNET #23   (June 4, 2018)

opposites converge at last in the eternal If
compact diversions of the mind asleep in its arm
let the shoulders do the knee and wrists fatigued
turn inside out the blood's skin seeking light

what others say can do the simplex attribute
syntax shorn of its individual hair the wild out
where once the isolate and peninsular together
girls outrunning porches foxfire the highway

traveling south with the dead which is the course
mountain slides and proportions of wind and
didn't it ever occur to overturn the rain a question

mark the significance of eternity in this blade
of grass with its fingers and so it goes twilight
in front of the abandoned house of yes infinity

SONNET #24   (June 4, 2018)

listening to the opera's Italian arias in reverse
singing the little bit of time left to breathe light
a skin of Mozart the genesis of sand & origins
of script within the eyelid stars and amazement

writing to you this profound hour it is dawn
in the Pleiades the asterisks are ablaze with loss
can I help it if tears and knees troubled with romance
schoolbooks and postulates of inveterate chaos

cannot go back to that room with its Neolithic
speech patterns phonetic decay oratorio and Hamlet
inscribed cities beneath the undertaker's fingernail

the first time will certainly be the last in a Spain
somewhere to the south of the cemetery where mothers
plead grievances of the long forgotten Trojan war

SONNET #25   (June 5, 2018)

in Sanskrit it's next year already they know
how to number even the forgeries bright red
constellations counting from one to eight and
then some a wave of galactic darkening a surf

spondees and trilogies of broken philologies
a half which is never an ideal circle revolving
in its hapless hemisphere of inks and homonyms
lightning too and comets asterisms it's too fast

it's a tongue running out of its mind it's writing
because that's life I told you once and then what
the sophists disagree on the terminology dying

settling little camps of punctuation Brahmins holy
star-gazers brothers in arms of an exfoliate myth
it's so rapid and the fade I cannot see past it

SONNET #26   (June 5, 2018)

running overtime with no escape from these
fourteen weeks the respirator the coagulation
of blood and moreover melancholy in its dry well
dots out of sequence with sadness in its almanac

put into a box and almost forgotten the named
survives in a fog of religious conjecture a shape
hovering above whatever it is ashes spell spilled
over the day's wasted patina of distant echo

similar to but not its equal in passion the heart
outruns itself and the definitions begin to pour in
cancelled rain the physics implicit in a cloudburst

to hide from the ancient weather a mixture of grass
and stain the monotony of windows traveling by
in order to get to the mortuary by this afternoon

SONNET # 27   (June 5, 2018)

heavy the thick and shaking remembrance in
the plural even worse turning to invoke the phantom
she isn't really there plasmic barely visible if she
revolves on the pedestal sentient marble plus

chill it gives even the thought going under like
that is a way to ending it a vision at a time her
on the edge as they say enticing through the ether
to move as if but no matter how she shimmers any

fixed in circulation barely an echo of glass the rain
if one could stop it forever the gravel underfoot
strikes the clock at four done with the burning

later driving around and the shroud too bright for
its pulse the amaryllis bursting feverishly red almost
out of the hands her presence a smoking text trails

SONNET #28   (June 5, 2018)

I will forever if not just now on the cusp of knowing
whatever could have been has and earth sodden
down turned the face of every man as if asking
will this be eternity were it not for the aching

moving in rows irregular through the bolgia shades
not men illuminated phrases quivering on the cave wall
hunters with bow and the pale of moon following
the slowly descending into the small whirlpool

milling hands in the darkening and the whispers
all but loud the fierce tone of rust in the ears
how is it twilight the unready finish of this day

first and last the minute has come the swirling anger
hair taken by grief and surprised the knees fall apart
who will not touch nor be touched the spirit ascending

SONNET #29   (June 5, 2018)

in all the world I know two *Arturos* and one *Rafael*
curtailed by the stop edging towards the vast empty
ox-cart trail fading off in the tangle of brute memory
inky smudges on each brow the terror not silence

in all the world there remains one cathedral
and two cups and the rain that fills them falling
for no more is minus one the other nor one hand
two fingers and three hemispheres the mere whole

fixed like the moon in its minor passage and Uranus
way out there signaling to have it all back no more
than I can you have you out of infernal promises

so be it road trips to the very south of the mountain
and the dust of every evening and the windfall and
there ! the unseen shore too many waves one drowned

SONNET #30   (June 5, 2018)

that each has its every and the day has yet to be
a solid confirmation shades quickening into
spirits lingering the longing which hour will it
be counting backwards in Siamese toward grief

the unwilling who despondent want to have
their grace of tea and moons circling feathered
brows the mythic quotient in the historical trap
mountain and slides and ungovernable reality

such as they are so we are as well holding on to
the meridian in unfulfilled cycles ever vanishing
of heat fields and rows of the unmown flashing

in a light all fall switching code the irreverent swift
how is a mind to recount aggravated minutes waiting
dispense with formalities phantom ego gone Poof !

SONNET #31 (June 5, 2018)

so what if I got the dates wrong the world's still
in conjunction sorrowing its otherness in spite
turned the collar up felt running the disk around
for the music to play and remote more whispers

unrecorded devices the mental tricks we play
you with your honorific pronouns *Usted* and *Vous*
and I somewhere between pyramid and algebra
a routine looking for its mask the piety of numbers

mismatch of evenings coming to the door ringing
who's home who's gone forever the room dark
with absence so many letters unsigned the role

if it weren't for the next day with its rooster dawn
and the market place with its hanging meat and
the ampersand and angel intertwined how would we ?

SONNET #32   (June 5, 2018)

misspelled undertaken rushing waters underneath
hands folded prayer-wheels and the red red wind
taking us by the hair back to a mineral sleep alone
can you feel me it asks rotating in its green verse

feel nothing but the projected hand and its wall
if only and what is always unsaid remains the night
voices calling back and forth echoing in the drain
come back it seems to shout but no ear alert stays

they are writing all that has to be determined blank
and auspicious on this day of irreverence and awe
the streets fill with the shadows of ash the whitest

please as to turn right on the semaphore disowning
that you have ever seen me and back off into dusk
every mountain has its spill can you feel me it asks

SONNET #33 (June 5, 2018)

beginning with number five can we say who's next
rock solid the mystery is only a lunation a gravity
a sense that it can never happen again the ship
sets off on its own planetary voyage a long lost

leaving from the onset a puzzle to shift aside
sleeping in the shape of ink as it stains slowly its
vast until morning finds us in the arm of memory
reticent to retell the narrative of rising quicksilver

heavens away from the moment of departure the soul
what was its body all about its named absences
its errant walks through deep and dark the wood unseen

it will never know and pausing to quiz its water a hand
it takes to pool a drink face down in the evanescent dark
waiting to hold and be held by *her* the phantom bride

SONNET #34   (June 5, 2018)

are there zeroes without complacency or a world justified
by its error ? you went to the dance alone what did
you anticipate a partner a mask a frame of reference ?
how did this death happen so sudden yet not unexpected ?

what cannot be identified is the finger lost at twilight
dusk growing in the grasses hard by the ancestral porch
a minimal cipher or a pyramid discovered on the equator
where oceans reach but never find their lone geography

coming home unbalanced unaccompanied but for a moon
already red in its diminishment began to understand right
the reason and its many longing for just a vowel to bind

undone it all came and the well and the uprooted tree of
memory all echo and no leaf spreading the dark intensity
being alive for that one moment all zeroes and no sight

SONNET #35   (June 5, 2018)

or if not a person some sort of identity playing out
the stage in a sequence of talking shadows irreverent
as statues in their trembling marble to speak aloud
in the otherwise darkness that shrouds being

a leaf accounted for a mower a section of wind painted
for its discrepancies to blow into the plunging waters
such as grief is wave piled upon wave in a small glass
mired in the deception of breath an afternoon of longing

smaller still the distances the hills separated by a comma
the unattainable horizon with its pinnacles of angst
no pill can reduce no balm reside the disquieting cloud

overturned by a simple mistake history multiplies itself
none can read aright what it says on the last pages
rock and stone caves of conjecture all a simple loss

SONNET #36   (June 5, 2018)

if it weren't for the child within where would
the elbow be ? and what about the knee how would
it find its cathedral in the dark ? how would fingers ?
a lengthened trace ink forever without memory

how would writing find its place beside oblivion ?
would shoulders bear resemblance to the Christ ?
logic reason and philosophy without the child within
could there be a stochastic process a freedom to deny ?

I lost the child within and walked without all day long
I spoke to adversaries of the light to foemen in disregard
dark was the denatured afternoon its long deluded hours

my elbows could not speak my knees no more could think
my shoulders denied salvation and my fingers lost in grass
logic reason philosophy nothing but running ink gone mad

SONNET #37   (June 5, 2018)

sweet landings on the moon obverse coins of sight
listen to the peahen dancing on its drum a song
we never heard the descant of a dreaded underside
the world a loss ! pennies and rags in glistening sun

so much for make believe the one is dead the two
no more and from three on down the man is gone
who wove his vowels of madness while we prattled
on the shore and moonlight undressed the sky

time is a thimble worn to the ceaseless bone of night
nothing fits a blade turning on its side of light alone
we wander loosened from the solitary key of sand

and dance to write the water of our life and search
the livelong day a marching tune drilled in our ears
blind instruments in the perplexity of our little death

SONNET #38   (June 5, 2018)

yet not know why the angel of assumptions
is at the door and knocking a cribbed darkness
of the soul a bright hour of the day just born
a hundred mantles color of tamarind descend

covers on both sides of grammar the unlearned
rules omega and affix of the root vowel puzzling
as it is inherent to waking this voluble morning
and listen to the door swaying toward the west

great hills ! where we will go come sundown
packaged with our punctuation and slow grief
millimeters of remaining light sorrowing disorder

someone is tracking the numinous way wooded
though intractable and the dank soil brimming with
voices of the dead incoherent as winding sleeves

SONNET #39   (June 5, 2018)

hold it the ribbon unraveling with its codes
held to the sun and your face beside it a length
of light and gone you turned into a statue of ink
could I but make repairs and the memory of

your last words before subsuming cold atmospheres
everything life has to offer goes like that in shifts
of color and disorganization standing by the door
the passenger entrance to the emergency room a

siren and a flock of birds scatters wildly in the air
just inches from the designations for spring and summer
in the window a goddess withdraws the remnants of sleep

you called out from a trance of caryatids carved
from the wounded marble that haunts inscriptions
in enigmatic and lacustrine syllables all fading

SONNET #40   (June 5, 2018)

it's Orpheus take a look holding something wet
ages since the rock wept he sat on it mourning
becomes a dove a flight of wings without gravity
look again and stanch the tears and grassy winds

cannot have back cannot possess the shadow of
slithering serpentine between his legs the lore
kenning insubstantial beauties wildly sung on
his ancient lute the deaths of all that moved

so to hospitals of glass and aerodromes built on
marsh and fen the entire west sinking beneath the sun
a twilight remorse a second and third attempt a

disappears like fade and absence in porphyry atone
hands give over to hands the pantomime of going under
sweet it's Orpheus all hair unkempt all voice gone

SONNET #41   (June 6, 2018)

could be the gods gone crazy with determination
auto-reflex mountain toppled pinnacle of algebra
schoolkids is all they are teasing goddesses and nymphs
bush and underbrush undressing what's left of skin

mow 'em down slide still the subterranean gas a
whiteside section three thirds sky and a fifth ammonium
ether and peninsulas of sea-breeze a brilliant tone
steeped in skin the bronze age luster of the Queen

all sash mascara eye-black polish listing lace undone
her is the one of Death purple shade antinomy and
mud pack come to run her dogs around the grill

if they won't give back what's the use of prayer
mill ponds greenish fade of rotting lotus leaves
here was the dear sailor last seen dissolved in light

SONNET #42   (June 6, 2018)

speaking as if sound could last and decay and airs
spun violence and cloudy acrimony the supernal
high on meth the tottering Zeus-thing his aghast
to make things worse earthlings gone to war again

what was to learn from all that bloody myth and
tripe the whetstone hidden in the garage the alcohol
shadows face down in peat as if reciting prayers
to the gods below the children missing from their paper

an altar a broken temple column rubble of oracular
jade jewelry the bracelets and thongs once adorned
could be talking about the haruspex or the terminator

prized animals sent flying into the sky my child too
pierced wings two hands lesser than the day of birth
hours of luminous absence everything come to naught

SONNET #43   (June 6, 2018)

equivalent of air fare to Corpus Domini price
of one hospital bed per diem the flagstones ruined
ruffled the sheets yellow with perspiration week long
in time the finalizations a quotient not promised

beautiful the angels invisible in their enormous flight
their song the harp-tones strings kettle drums and sistra
come back ! the mantra enchantment of voices by the
dozens alarms and hosannas alike the baleful note

driving over and over the afternoon's turnpike hard
by the volcanic map and here it was the designated
such as it could ever be ethereal fragile a loss forever

held hand wept deep stone mourning words fraught
template woven from skies of impossibility the tender
mind what was left and the gradually ascending smoke

SONNET #44 (June 6, 2018)

hard to see past the margins unfolding the testament
blown winds from the far south amber colored suns
duplicate rising from the mountain's Sanskrit text
why couldn't it be averted this moment by the threes

afterwards someone will be in touch however aggravated
stones lifted wells dug ditches planned mortuary walls
cyclopean in distance erected as a warning to the heavens
here was laid to rest so and so with his culpable knees

noon so swift comes and goes in cups of cyanide and
why didn't they translate exactly what they meant
when they said don't go past the Pyramid of the Moon

the hour ! at least fifty minutes longer than expected
shirts on backwards sleeves muffled at the wrists pulse
no longer measures its intricacy of hives and light

SONNET #45   (June 6, 2018)

to go beyond the poem all too mortal a tenuous fiction
vibrations intimations divinations sea-wrecks marooned
madness of the survivors on their granite outpost who
will listen to this recitation of citadel and ominous ruin

tensions ! a face from out of nowhere and hexameters and
a Sabine farm deep into the night inscribing verses in a
mirror that only reads from right to left augurs and poets
scattered on the playing field ghosts and specters vanished

what is to ink in this missing self portrait but a few words
cataloged for their errors and misgivings I never meant it
anyway this deceptive coronary of clouds and gods in mufti

turn off all the lights ! here and here the squiggles of text
the dead were right nothing lasts not even the greatest art
to reveal the famous nullities a phrase *the Big Bang* ! AOI

SONNET #46   (June 6, 2018)

we are aspiring to be clouds bright framework
still unachieved is the stellar labyrinth too far to reach ?
remember the day in the schoolyard the voices
of pure distance small ethers of dust a chance to die

that was when it started to go the range of efforts a
pulse in the grass heart beats like the tom-tom of the west
what an imagination and the bluffs and rivers winding
through everything that is steep and inaccessible

one by one the heavens ! but to be clouds ? put on
your shoes tighten your belt patch your pants here
a comb for the time when out of step with the others

you happen to fall and the moons how many of them in
your eyes the vast and insignificant of outer space a light
the dizzy and cerebral trying to speak and cannot why

SONNET #47   (June 6, 2018)

shouldered the sound consonants in profusion utterance
monumental carved from pure memory the air a bright
and struggle to retain just a third of it put down writing
how swiftly dismembered the words what it was going

to say and light shedding across the moving leaves
breeze rippling green assonance almost liquid gold
melting on the tongue are we blind to let it go ? sweet
hummingbird and asterisk things blown into the immense

dear as dust you are fossil phantom faint tracing a name
was it ever yours how it echoed in the lattice sleeping
darksome thing a legend writ in argent liquid threads

at last come home wrapped in something other than
how hush the moons varied in their diminishing phase
look up there and read the pale semblance of your body

SONNET #48   (June 6, 2018)

everything was so tenuous a delirium you could hear
the helicopters like a circular thought alone buzzing
a relic a husk a what a fever was coming on then
yellow nothing out there on the gravel some steps

who come to be wary and pull the switch life could be
otherwise satin sashes shades drawn the unmoving
behind the wall a city hauled out of the lake the dense
activity of ants carving a red hieroglyph in stone

making a wheel with wings of water the sensuous high
being like a demonized skin without a soul craving an
identity a mask a cicatrix of mind a dizzying undone

each hand a text of mobility searching for its other
darkening veins that open and shut the gate *beyond*
fingers groping rings of dust anemones of the unknown

SONNET #49 (June 6, 2018)

reading is what gives a thought to it the ancient
warped half-lost text to puzzle over intent and design
here was what they meant by blood and on the overleaf
the illustration in faded blank of the origin of space

it's not meant for us to understand nor to give the arm
its test for flight if wings were shoulders and tomorrow
the stone we must overcome if we want to push ahead
schemes are borderlines sand and ink the enigmas

write me when you get there let me know the waters
whether they separated when the oracle darkly spoke
and if night is as eternal as the grasses said it would be

never finished the book put it aside beside the caryatids
black wax leaves of rivers uncontained swarms of light
dust is migration of the soul numbers cannot be determined

SONNET #50   (June 6, 2018)

half way to the end less than a third of the way to paradise
stepping stones dark hallways where the body can be
unknown levels of thought a fourth of the way back
no direction unless it's south the unmarked path home

frail bark on life's tossed seas am I to survive the next
by wounds haunted the dying to the light the unnumbered
why is escape preferable ? kindred spirit in its room
without walls lacking doors outside is forever within

bare feet slapping wet clay dancing unconscious the only way
lotus-eyed soul wafting in yards of red silk bearing winds
planets glass fish triangles tingling an entire jungle of noise

when we stop rotating when we wake up three days later
in the Intensive Care Unit beside the prophet when the call
for the recognitions at last summons the borderline of mind

SONNET #51   (June 7, 2018)

the celestial phenomena and what they call
Throne-of-the-Gods we were late observing
nor did our fragile bark tossed between cliff
and cliff withstand why should we not have

then and there died spume and star disoriented
what goes under at the last nor survives matter
be it wood or rust and the curved empyrean above
what could language avail small prayers begging

what like meteors or comets whiplashed flames
fate predicting moments in ignorance experienced
divine fire-works nerve and suture the oncoming

end a trellis of torn fabric withering vine summer
heat spells the whole cycle of life-events curtailed
in the least of the moon-falls on our knees weeping

SONNET 52 (June 7, 2018)

could from such a childhood of mansions and grass
the evidence of tragedy such as Aristotle devised
five acts with music by Mozart and index finger
rotating round the temple grown old in a day

me you see never as before wishing for the critical
event to strip these lengthening days neither festive
nor heat-spilled and lay the body down in its feather
bed inquiring of the dark that spells the mind

is this what mother wanted is this the fiction of time
great legendary scripts to be read on the ceiling a
glass of pure alcohol and the conversation with Bacchus

rise up from your knees ! this is no mere shipwreck
on the coast of Cyrene nor the abyss in the backlands
searching noon after noon for the Deus-ex-Machina

SONNET #53   (June 7, 2018)

OK you say let's go over this one more time where
were you the night of and what were you doing so
behind the ruins of Astarte's temple out there
in the sands the endless complexity of sky detritus

the fortune teller and the palm reader and the augur
what did they know of the Irreversible ? hungered
for truth discarded the scientific explanations fate
immolated on this rock where mourning you sit days

nothing accounted for the sheets spread out to dry
listening for the voice to issue from the one great cloud
above and the birds circling with human cries the heavens

exactly as summers are and bound to end experiencing
the muffled rot the dense greenery can barely breathe
asking over and over what is that unexplained streak

SONNET #54   (June 7, 2018)

will not and extend series of words wild vocables imprecations
suppliant vowels one two and no more than three incidents
in the broken grammar of the testaments exhausting human
nerve crying with both knees announcing what cannot be

look and respond and open the door and gravitate darkly
on either side a symbol you cannot resist and shut down
the grasses spearheads of minute accidents the crashing ire
could not have been more surprised the yellow pinwheels

spinning in the eyes the mental consonants like ores shining
for the instant only before and as always reading scripture
the gods who did this and that the failed interruptions

such as the entrance to death is a peninsula extending its
wishes into the phantom and archaic sea that fills the ear
roaring silences the poetry of the immense and ineffable

SONNET #55   (June 7, 2018)

so it isn't a translation but the original in mimeograph
a memory a recollection a fault line a confession in omega
sigmatic aorist imprecations the invisible text corrupted
by scribes who later it is usually the case dust bound oriental

mistakes typos misplaced accents the whole a debacle
illegible ink splotches squiggles dots and some kind of most
likely the cause if not phonetic decay at its worst a saddening
remnant on the margins like birds drawn by a palsied hand

you will attempt a lecture extracting from the sky clouds
and apply to the eye a caustic and water the beds of lotus
and wait quite simply for the meaning to gravitate a night

when with insomnia the mind you are starts buzzing incoherent
bees in mid-air puzzling what you mean starting from a dream
can you ever find the key it is not too late the door shuts

SONNET #56   (June 7, 2018)

the tragic bloom Narcissus drowned in the negative
curvature of space iridescent in its time exposure
to the fatal light when come down all the windows
a sash drawn over the spreading pool of night

didn't you as well recount the tale retold a thousand
times in the waiting room magazine covers displayed
with the latest accidental star and touch-ups fading
the once color of such life the wild and potentially

whatever the call for orders and the clock on the wall
stuck at the very moment of the volcano and airs
ashen filled and in the glass the trapped latin insect

just so memory fails to bring back texture and outline
the face as recalled in its sublime lineaments bright
but for the rest stained rusted a moon of its former self

SONNET #57   (June 7, 2018)

what is love but a tale of displaced persons
temperatures gone wrong running hot and cold
mercury and the planets out of orbit chasing
dust-storms in pianissimo lotus fragrances

recounting numbers that don't add up nights
witches' Sabbath when eyes distort the Seen
bringing moon down to the seas and shores of
destroyed cities holding tryst with ivy subterfuge

don't demean the lovelorn capsized in a thimble
of prussic acid or devoured by the big omega of
molten gold with seizures and complex orgasms

you and I bidden to the courts bewildered and stray
numinous head-hunters prowling phonic distances
we have lost everything not only the zero but the OM

SONNET #58 (June 7, 2018)

the remote the recondite subterranean unconscious
ultimately hands to the hold and rushing crazy waters
bearing sleep away the forever of index fingers pointing
to broken boat sails and winds and riggings beckoning

come home it says on the dotted line bestir and ink
erasures of the Office unconditional surrender death
agencies browning in the hills always the fading plural
smitten by a memory that never happened on the sun

wounds and disorder of ore and mineral and enormous
the saying of disbelief aphasic and dementia pleading
that light be disturbed no more nor breathing the accident

it will be written somewhere else how the throne was adorned
jewelries the pearl bed antinomies lacking any syntax until
juxtaposed to lunations and hemicycles life itself undone

SONNET #59   (June 7, 2018)

breathing backwards like a knife on the cusp of being
burning pages faster than a life comes into the light
surrounding airs mothering tenderly the happening
what a marvel and to own nothing and to fly upwards

a wondrous moment in its reversal caught by the camera
eye a hundred circumstances just like it called identity
grounded on sands of sleep reiterated in the flicker of
an instant all of space textures of invisible punctuation

you cannot nor should you try to remember exactly
and when the bullet and the kite and the echo splendid
reach that point in time known as self awareness then what

nothing can be gathered out of the waters of oblivion
you slip into a coma you release from the hands a script
that you should have read but forget to being dazzled

SONNET #60   (June 7, 2018)

such as it is the book never took shape a chapter
at a time erased no sooner come to consciousness
a lamp shining on the unnumbered parts and water
marks spoiled decisions to cancel and white-out

going to bed to re-read the day's unremembered
activities you are never sure of yourself nor that you
even spelled any of the words correctly sounding out
brief syllables of desperation and oracular defeat

never mind the next day if it comes is always new fresh
unbidden yet dangerous as well strangers will be there
not to reassure but to question intent and denial

difficult to locate the door retrace steps use hands as if
you knew what they were a clause stuck in the brain of
luminous meaning but what precisely you don't know

SONNET #61   (June 8, 2018)

? and the mysterious depths unkenned solitary out
there bi- or tri-partite hemispheres involving light
disappearance of the inchoate and misunderstanding
were you ever sure it was tomorrow when the sun

sideways as it moves over sand mounds ever increased
power to heat and regenerate and lost you think not
linking task to cause and reason to distance a disaster
in language shifts from red to organic breathing less

easy now the ward's closed-door policy registered
in pinnacles of ampersands sliding off ? exclaimed !
grammar and disorientation morphology of the unknown

switch off the motors dim the lights hold still face down
memory slowly going out like gas through a sieve
colder still the concrete abutment where you lie waiting

SONNET #62   (June 8, 2018)

such as life is today a traffic of speed and heat
nothing retained in the pupil a gas of thoughts
exploding simultaneously like gods of counterpoint
words in snatches of diatribe and threnody

cannot hold on to the meaning cannot understand
there is nothing to it but go under into the morass
shorten the breath quicken the step flood the eye
sand-trap vertigo death knell drumbeat ecstasy

pharaohs in their endless noon an ear to the sun
elided vowels symphonies of parasitic consonants
enormous conflagrations within the parading inch

give marble its chance to become a sarcophagus
tender incisions in the breath of moon night downs
its wings snapped in two a heave ho ! dust the myriad

SONNET #63   (June 7, 2018)

ills of language letting go of the rest sliding out from
resolutions to sleeping the god-head in its rock solid
upheaval will we ever they ask all the physical world
you inhabited writing verse after fondly attaching a

speaking closely to the ground listen intently the murmur
divinities sectioning the spoils of the Unconscious between
worlds and the immense and sad suddenly gone by a
mere telephone call no reviving speech nor breath

limitless what happens afterwards and they shut off
the lights a marvel to just be there a husk of air
how to control the sobbing in sheets layered like clouds

it is brief to be inscribing and then up looking a sound
was it from dying to wake this door a simple fragment
opening on what is even vaster of the universe alone

SONNET #64   (June 8, 2018)

she it was excited the knob in the other hand the right
self or maybe less than the reddish hue a blush roses
highlighting memory of its hotel the few quarters
unlit and looking back darker than recalled a fuse

when no one responded and turned the flashlight
into a corner dim the geometries she was confused
batteries they inquired and for a while the rustling
behind glass the quarantined thoughts of ending it

what's to pretend the elements neatly on the chart
color infused with emotional difficulties to translate if
there is an assertion the shepherd on his monumental stone

twining reeds to invent the pan's pipe and sit rocklike
the picture of mourning in the abstract whitening music
the afterword don't mention it a face without its mirror

SONNET #65   (June 8, 2018)

more and more syntax an egress of thought imploded
seeking reason to cause skies and askew the thunder
shaking like an agony of dust storming the western
with its eclipse of hills come twilight the longing green

and promise this is the last and will be shedding light
before night falls on the myth of water the steep cliff
with its pronoun of impersonality you are talking now
what seems its eternity of an echo to return tomorrow

and what is being said into the megaphone a city listens
but summer isn't quite right in the bend rushing dreams
the kids somehow lost tousled hair buttoned wrongly shirts

pick out to the right the photograph near its center fading
each of them used to be alive with their model speech
yet the one who was dead from the start yes behind him

SONNET #66   (June 8, 2018)

mostly dark now can still echo the hearing in the stone
like an ear yet to be explored for its canals of rust asleep
canvas and stars shooting out the fire hydrant muzzled
and their feet bare from the hip down wildly silent

chewing gum talks snapping back a memory and depth
we all must die we all will die it's just a reverie sweet
and impassive near the old grocery store where the nickel
invented for its fossil activity and place a hand inside

meant to be read when you get home this letter sent I
from afar it was fondly the shape sun sets took writing
before the hills in their absence grew darker still

put the head heavy down before sleep shares its alpha
with the now missing planet a dream they declare finite
as ink which can never wake and we miss you terribly

SONNET #67   (June 8, 2018)

King Arthur with his battleships of corrosive lilies
will sing evening's great sinking a ballad hushing
of twilight and porphyry the beauties of a gone world
we are listening for its unfolding ribbons and sadness

voices issuing from rock and rock in its soundless depth
who can tell the difference ? the dead in their trees
mocking shadows of light but forgetting the liberty
of speech and restless to find ears and to understand

hours of unsurpassed sublime choirs accompaniments
of grass and tubular horizons the melancholy chimes
that mark day's titular passing in downgrades of red

so if darker comes and it's only night's awful substitute
death ! scatter then the colons and commas the peripheries
of the lamp as it rings circles around the drowning hand

SONNET #68 (June 8, 2018)

what is whiter than yearning blanched throat
pulse beating slender blue as cyanide more tender
than blush longing the fleet image gone was alive
and like winds making of branches a map of desire

can speak into the dark sleeve echoes memory's
fleet tongue unraveled sound the archaic in stone
hidden as the labyrinth of myth come out rushing
from pools a water deep as night the unthought

softens breath unties laces listing bankside into
primitive lakes elevated into the ether a film darkening
of gone afternoons the surface a summer in length

and hear no more in crevices of distance the aching
inks staining unconscious satins the arm extends
into what pronominal galaxy of mind hitherto unknown

SONNET #69   (June 8, 2018)

it isn't what is constructed but what it destroys
leaving each margin the whiter for its afterthought
shipwreck in an instant and what plunges deep
into the submerged inky all hands loss of mind

come with me Little One the worst has been and
to the left of the picture to the far side of the image
waters propelling wings heights or rock and cloud
a few remaining gods Look ! alighting on pastures

of azure and sympathy resemblances to the gone
whom do we have now to mourn ? they trumpet sad
illusory scenes in the hills of a quiet occidental sepia

temple shakings columns in despair of acanthus and ivy
twining round the head less heavy now its sleeping down
a recollection of green canals of plastic cities of toys

SONNET #70   (June 8, 2018)

no expression remains it goes under so swiftly
darksome the reaches into billowing dreams the
surf caps of missing identities a form of weighing
air and its myriad substitutes in the near future

it wasn't Achilles the brooding shadow on the main
nor Orestes wrapped in thunderheads and furious
to have at the proximate suburb of *dramatis personae*
the willful lengthening of speech into archaic stone

everything is one and the single leaf and unmown grass
the strictures of a parenthesis on trial for its reddening
unwritten consonants alphanumeric prestidigitation

a miracle we are sitting here in the stitching to marvel
at the passage of thread through the eye the punctuated
hiatus of life play-acting characters from zero to zed

SONNET #71   (June 8, 2018)

reducing thought to its circular origins what are we
gnomic utterances fled from the mid-day stage
noon time ears listening for the counter ploy a plot
to destroy recognition and soon it is the rainstorm

intermezzo and nostalgia for thunder and rock high
to the left of the vast scenario painted on zephyrus
his breezy locks and mountains of sudden lifted
to portray this Grecian tragedy of mad minimalists

that's the you and the I and the unknown other fleet
as sands blowing across her lacking sea and speeches
wrought from iron balustrades and the itself of memory

come to this day and settle here your downy quilt and sit
a while catch your breath it's long before the lake and its
ridges the western hills where death plans its stratagems

SONNET #72 (June 8, 2018)

so quiet and lay the other his design and multiple puzzle
this is the sleep predicted by the oracle and its words
never to be fathomed a baffle of unwritten consonants
the Sybil in her glassy fit trying as ever to speak her stone

do such lands come to us and shorelines buffeted by alien
the tavern to the right of midline a rhetoric of prophesy
where we drink to the dregs our doom-say rioting archaic
'til twilight finds us shoulder to shoulder with death unexpected

assume to rectify yesterday's quoits missives darted at a wall
flares of conduct shifts from deepest red to the darker Sicily
of rock and windblown gusts of grass and memory alike

what is oblivion to this touch of drowse here in the steep
gathering what can of the blustery and waves below we dare
knowing ill the passage that betrays us to night's eternity

SONNET #73   (June 8, 2018)

too soon and gone the way to speak the sounding
loud for once and day's disquieting slips away
forever silence to reign where once the blustery
a city or the squadrons of memory and myth

couldn't we have better the light to have known
the air to breathe its rust and oxided histories
writing when we could the diaries to forget alone
night's unaware dreamt and forbidden the flight

to other spaces aloft the then and never of the past
you were a sight gamboling on the meadow fair the green
sloping into and out of consciousness the great unknown

but to always have let slide the hand away from its grip
rounded earths circles that cannot be drawn in grass
the leaf of wind the doorway at the top the heavens

SONNET #74 (June 8, 2018)

can one be dead for only fifteen weeks and count
backwards to the moment of activity in the already
dark the rich night extending its yawning to before
space and the groping crab nebula and the moon !

why is it we are unable to spell correctly the meanings
doom swift chants ricocheting in the stone's left ear
smoothing out the creases air leaves as it abandons
once and for all the shapes each hand creates alone

definitions are for the unready the ones who come
afterwards to investigate something of the cavity
which is earth inchoate the blowing away into time

it is us poor souls holding texts of erased cuneiform
dotting and speculation of what went before repeating
what Echo cannot remember the unutterable say

SONNET #75   (June 8, 2018)

was it Mandrake the Magician who told us
Inferno was three doors down from the last exit
but if you want to go to Paradise he advised
you must cut in half the breath it takes to get there

being and saying so thinking only makes it a dream
the opposites of number cannot contain becoming
one is on the shore and the other nowhere to be found
alas illusions only illustrate the windows of disbelief

how there can be so little time to remember what
he said standing aloof in his cape on the rock of solitude
magnificent shimmer of bluish ink his impeccable top hat

tomorrow if you turn the page the horizon inhabited
now by nocturnal birds and the long withheld Dawn he said
will in an instant vanish beyond the category of light

SONNET #76   (June 8, 2018)

the thus fulfilled vaticination the alembic and root
la curandera who draws back the black and red curtains
who dons a rainbow plumage dancing barefoot like
a partridge and thunders resound and skies spit yellow

seeds rain the shallows filling and cannot more seized
trees become whispers ancient and leaf and rock amaze
wherever was earth now seas shoreless wave on wave
the roiling surf with its uncounted and hidden moons

there dreaming we the invisible unborn travel mighty
when will we ever inhabit the body again when turn from
sleep the talking legends we have read about in the palms

wake ! it ever was a semblance light wavering between crests
imitations of land loud as moving cliffs across the vacancies
will we know one and the other in our longing former selves ?

SONNET #77 (June 8, 2018)

starting from the seasons the various and sounding
against barriers of space the undefined quarters
spreading from memory and music the wordless
sewing invisible threads the Fates sad in their perspective

each allotted a kind of life letters signs an echo half
a dream sections diminishing of light to wonder
was this me I was born to and this hill when did I
climb it before and the houses of darkness all around

so spinning through the night activities that separate
man from woman and the whole undivided sphere
circling the ear of the unsuspecting mortal whoever

conscious of nothing but the advance of days that just
as soon disappear tilting off the shelf and distance the
being in so many colors that cannot sustain its weight

SONNET #78   (June 8, 2018)

it is come to an end this hand now a fog of distances
nothing felt nor the insistence to return the breath
holding back other frontiers of light freighted tones
that seem to gyrate mysteriously above the grieving

if we set off driving again down the missing pike
avoiding as ever the exits that detain the weary soul
aiming straight away for the brow of a dreaming god
and secure to find somehow there is another Side

etched in air notches of thought knots tightening sight
the eye undone by its own electric fish a radiance
that dazzles even the sun with all its dialectic homophones

it is the pronoun that hurts most the knees it sustains
the gravity it keeps from swaying too much by weight
and finally its own definition ethereal ego otherness

SONNET #79   (June 8, 2018)

is there any place ever nearer that it's
not the farthest place by night ? where
latitudes finally meet somewhere in space
the undeveloped photo finds its light

stuttering hands cautious beam wavering
so alone drifting down the dividing line
between what had been and what is recalled
the echo in its multiple hemispheres a fade

soon it is darkness in hills of intense yearning
where we go frequently afternoons on the wane
yesterday's houses one by one the undetermined

can no longer find the forehead or its metal shade
thinking breaks down to a spear and aims where
least the heavens separate their tremulous fours

SONNET #80   (June 8, 2018)

no other poem but this unwinding grammar
of the road and its bifurcations the time of
the envelope unbidden hush the mystery sign
decorated the sleeper with gravel and silence

when the reading is half way and the teacher
looks up from her flotilla of adverbs it's three
already hour of the bell and the puzzled shepherd
outside the slopes are greening the darkest part

what's called home what takes part in ceremonies
numbers of indivisible atomic theory sun storms
aching to find out the score even before it begins

racing sideways water from the rushing wall spouts
who can remember the first line of the epic memory
lying there in the hospice life of the Buddha recited

SONNET #81   (June 8, 2018)

can so much of the day have elapsed its stolen
hour of uncounted minutes waking up by the tree
where slept for two hundred of them an error
in reverse the winding sheet slowly descending

a cloud in the battlements shouting the wild gesture
if it had hands to wield and to save itself from it
a divinity for sure wrapped around the ore of light
instilling a chill in the uninstructed by the roadside

soon there will be no distance only the instantaneous
inch the rain of fire the moving murals of packaged air
a tumult in the veins called life the needle scours for more

lie there don't move the thing won't be taking so rise
for what the river edge and watch the boulder smoothed
a voice listening to itself in the unshaken leaf of dew

SONNET #82   (June 8, 2018)

more so the enigma of words behind a screen of
fireflies capturing night with their tiny wings
almost as if whispering human girls their secrets
but cannot see what the contour of ink is in the heat

course of summer in its mythic parallel one June
that passed in a silent catastrophe the whole idea
spinning out of control fever embolism cataract hue
the mind sustaining all the gravity of the universe

before ominous the parade of names flitting like gods
waiting to control tomorrow with its sparrows of light
treetops zinging wild with the puzzle of the winds

taking your hair and surprise that the pool is not fuller
where yearning to ache the face is still there paling
the fade of consciousness and untied thoughts to drown

SONNET #83   (June 8, 2018)

refrains tidings conscious salutes from the other Beyond
that lives are not corpuscles nor little red anemones
fleshlets of dripping memorizations of light on earth
not the market plazas all huzzah and untethered horses

nor the porches of nostalgia their radios abuzz with
latest songs about gossip and news disasters and wild
loud and anxious what can never be rightly communicated
the heart's solo effort to fly through escape hatch centrifuges

out to the peninsulas where inscripted ruins frazzle hills
sculpted but fractured ovals of memory in Italian or Hindi
columns erected to the many true gods on the way long gone

powders of effusion and nights vast and unending heat
intaglios shattered cameos portraits in miniature that ply
the soul's abandoned canals cathedrals in dusky flight !

SONNET #84   (June 8, 2018)

early upanishadic speculation the world an upside
down tortoise or a maddened elephant rutting throngs
to hell with the puny mortal crushed underfoot the
juggernaut running loose in the torpid jungle streets

of this to rites of script of unending verses kings seers
wasp-waisted goddesses in a stew over dead paramours
concerts of tabla and sitar that last islands of time
high on opium mountain thousands of units in the mask

red and certainly violence associated with that color crash
anklets and earrings stolen from Vishnu dazzling bling-bling
and a hop and a jump to asterisms of exotic flare sleeping in

sleeves of cathay silk a million light years away just floating
fog of Mind ! just so are we teeter-tottering on the edge of
the abyss mere reflections in the imagined mirror of Brahma

SONNET #85   (June 8, 2018)

hand me the glass the perfumed rag the dotted hat and
a reader in ancient old Neolithic poetry nothing appears
to seem what it really is and a trip to the hospital doesn't
make it otherwise and in mourning grieving this millennium

for what must have been a dream a trick of the wrist as
first applied in magic halls the audience multiplied by
alcohol and meth driven to imaginations of infernal heat
bring him back ! clear the stage spread out fresh linen

does nothing have substance ? are you the one ? or the other ?
fashion show of delicate hues of a misinformed mind of
a germination of hemispheres imploding inside a lunar text

the next time there will be no counting past three in the great
continuum of dark matter a physics of sub-sub atomic parts
where identity is resolved in a patina of dissolved astral light

SONNET #86   (June 9, 2018)

the emptiness of the house unreality of hours three
at a time the subdivisions growing out of sleep
where land used to be and the bees as always
creating an afternoon of nostalgia of distant hives

such as it is life's continuity seems to proceed through
a city of undisclosed maps and the sight of the Bridge
once so dear in its window of oriental complexities
now a cause for unsustainable grief to never cross it

we have explored as if in a trance the great waters
where nothing reflects back the mysterious passage
the shoals reefs undiscovered islands the lure of naiads

nevertheless and it is always some conjunction or other
prevents us from understanding the variable syntax of ink
spelling rooms and slants and strange formations of hands

SONNET #87   (June 9, 2018)

to have sent forth condolence letters errors of sorrow
in a forgotten latin akin to the epistles gods write when
deceiving for all posterity the minutes spent on earth
and have no response but an enormous lunar silence

am I or am I not the pronoun that feels down to the knees
the grammatical shape haunting the ears of sleep or am I
simply the vertiginous divinity who by accident has driven
the car off the cliff into the arms of an enigmatic water

no matter the day's numbers are out of order a month
has elapsed since this morning and the boat is tossed
infernally by waves that have yet to reach the bottom

the incident of the recording device the music on the edge
songs of darkness elusive lyrics as if stolen from stone
am I to make of these the sequence of sublunar sonnets ?

SONNET #88   (June 9, 2018)

asterisks and opium perfumes of memory death
make it mine ! shifting from past to present tense
causing the future to collapse into an oral vision
why doesn't the language conform to its chaos ?

am the bitter me a dot dot dot of red and ampersand
does me have to ankle itself to a darker pool of the
and what do them have to do with heights of blood
stitching that numbers among virtues its other

the is not and me speaks louder in sleep and hiatus
is the best part the gravid reflex of a pronoun out of
step with itself me and them and you the awful other

please as to write back mother lost as you are and been
these momentous centuries since you passed a field away
now is time to pack it in me and the consequences of it

SONNET #89   (June 9, 2018)

pearls stolen from the god of gravity ! numberless
and the words to describe the impossibilities of a
text composed in sand and the Pharaohs of mexico !
guard against an overcautious traffic and noon time

it can't speak anymore but through statues posing
as childhood the immense and crying back for stone
walking through heat and weeping in arms of grass
that fills evenings with a terrible avuncular sadness

have we lost our relatives have the roads to Southland
been blocked by a mnemonic system of dope crazed angels
on our knees praying daily to our painted Guadalupe of time

and rosaries spinning through fingers a gesture of x-rays
vitriolic and small the leering deities of incomprehension
what can ever bring to bear on the organization of light ?

SONNET #90   (June 9, 2018)

what is salvation but the suspension of elbows
the registry of fingers on the cusp of ink the blow
to glass hegemonies circulating in afternoon heat
or a Sicily that can no longer be reached by boat

singing doesn't make it so the immense and circular
inches that separate life from breath the ovations
and incandescence of Olympians who couldn't care less
that we drive our mortal vehicles without wheels

using a language of stone-cutters to define our options
that exist on the left margin only and sawing down to
size the paper of our roles unable to speak for the statues

that litter this weightless moment with their mad appeals
to a justice system that ignores the shape of the hour
as never before I am but a footnote to an unknown text

SONNET #91 (June 9, 2018)

the common-places and fac-similes of the sonnet form
heat the excessive mountain storm tossed cliffs lovers
at sea and cold and rivers deep the ruins of Rome where
shepherds sit mourning rock and stone and grass alike

Naples and Venice the marriage of Harmony and Mercury
what are these to say texts of superscript & cryptic letters
heights and unreturning age youth can never be walls
no foot can hand to destiny hails and thunders bewailing

come part this way and lead to death the imminent sound
echoes the paling adjective its mourning loss of will and what !
write below tear stains the pillow of constant grief alone

some day no more will come an ending to language and fate
the Sisters Three at their wheel the hairs of mortals mourn
me too tossed to the side the errant and archaic ditch of memory

SONNET #92   (June 9, 2018)

a few more sentences ply the furious sea of doubt and
night its spell the fast held to the unanchored thought
lesser still the parenthesis that holds moon a captive girl
and chance elides its opium through asterisk and ink

come away then pretty ones the poem has no more to say
tongues that once spoke dream a talk of marble to dispel
robes of wind buttercup and daffodil spill to darkened airs
sky is gone clouds undone mountains of distant atmosphere

why walk we here between drugstore and book the afternoon
pages unread the smaller signals red and fading ampersands
schools have disappeared and mounds of memory irrevocable

syntax and semaphore lights blinking on and off but echoes
a remote hieroglyph sent spinning like a comet into outer space
what we have unlearned to write with missing fingers fate

SONNET #93   (June 9, 2018)

tears with this legend its script inspires a breathing
now inchoate an ink that eyes a dissolving lunar state
remarks how distance captures its lens in a brief letter
alpha and sigma and always delta's small blue irises

canst Thou ? immersed in memory's bitter flux a tongue
raveled by its self a thing to disown by these numbed
catastrophes to wit the unexpected charnal house of fate
the lapse and slip of meadows and incarnations dire

once is too many ago the tale it couldn't tell again before
how many did you recall counting on ten fingers all twelve
the dozen times it takes and then fell to agonies sublime

to bed then to sheets that cannot unfold to coldness and
dumb speech a mind halved by its sweet longing to ever cease
and herein lies the spell of heavens never to be reached

SONNET #94   (June 9, 2018)

is gone the shadow its heat shaped outline on the walk
come to noon with its siren sound great echo of heat
of islands and languages known only to the drowned
how must be vast the sun above to take away so much

yes and powders red and blank and volcanoes like
cities built on furnaces of myth the immense of sleep
the dreaming ochre hills of fate the entire occident
all too fading like pearls of pale and iridescent night

is fast the found and lost the smallest of earthly grounds
you slept there you woke you played its bells of grass then
you slept again in beds that moved through great cavities

cannot tell why you did not come back why some asterism
filled with toys of light and dark and moving hands that
talked and feet that of themselves had no need to be

SONNET #95 (June 9, 2018)

dichotomies of space reorientations fundamentals
poetry wingless its head light with feathery airs
no feet with which to travel only the obligation
to bear fruit to be shared these many times over

will anyone listen to the echoes ever fading
whose one time grace is sorrow rooted in depths
cannot come back and open wide the windows
in search of air the lightless burden of time

counting forwards through clouds of anomie
spirit pales mountains of vast invisibilities where
dwell the muses god-spent their eyes loud with Beauty

and yet and yet and yet moving through mortal grief
the plateaus where still the vicissitudes of breath
linger at quarrel with nothing less than fading day

SONNET #96 (June 9, 2018)

away with such illusions of verse and meter the dun
and pallid hill the far beyond of nymph and bard
alone bereft the poem to itself recites the end it is
the unfulfilled the missing lines the water marks

picks up the pen sets down to silence the rhyme of
never what no beginning had and unraveling love
aspires to fretwork of unheard music the very lyric
pause to hear and remember nothing but its echo

yellow fields spreading greenswards toward what's
bitter living sounds each letter then buried head
the heavy in softness outside the senses of the light

such will be what is recalled nights come so swift like
knives of sand the airs dividing and moon a voice all blanch
shedding its uncommon luster on waters of oblivion

SONNET #97   (June 9, 2018)

persistence of echo mineral sleep depths coming back
through fluorescent clocks will it ever be the same
discharge of hours vitreous eerie to wake listening
to the stranger in the next room discoursing with reason

how the heights are worn and the once mighty peaks
and valleys submerged and the earths that circled
triumphantly other sources of light now petty disks
so argued the stranger and yet we kept sleeping

logic and meaning small fobs on the Wheel a distance
with voices indiscernible mingling their ear with light
can't you hear them the multiple shapes of echo ?

is returned to the bankside where they spread to dry
sheets and the ancient myths a writing undone by rains
by spells of heat and finally the aftermath of thought

SONNET #98   (June 9, 2018)

sun ! thou great Beast ! heat in quotients of elevens
the human still on his knees rotating prayers Ah
and his backside a map of terrors and his lungs
will they ever exhale again and the walls all around

closing in the living space by inches from the ground
here it was I first and then a flood of questions my
head roared the filling of the airs and much I made
of the book and its illustrations of immense Light

planets of disregard ! holy ! the incomplete everything
a language of bone and thistle a graveside of luminosities
mourners in their brains of aphasia looking for the Word

waists of wind wrapping tomes of air around a remaining
vowel could mortal speech defy the rays and revolving
a hand in search of its fingers in the verdigris of time

SONNET #99   (June 9, 2018)

cannot think to write again the anatomy of light
a dirge or perhaps right the ecstasies of sound
making loud the former silence the encrypted
syllable making its way through the frail worm

a head does and dancing shakes the polar vowel
insistence of sacerdotal rites invokes the high !
insects twining alphabets of ivy in a twilight loam
do hills then echo as I once did the fevered tone ?

sing then the sinking wave its ebb and darkened tide
take away the shore in couplets of heroic sands alas
'tis Troy again to fall by memory's unwritten hand

I am as you were the one to pen these strokes alive
harmony in a wedding to all the stars in death so bright
come again breathe into these spaces the famous Eye

SONNET #100   (June 9, 2018)

by simply saying so words do not survive for still
on its cold stone the body no more implores its shade
we have come home again and again a routine broken
by its own repetition reopen then the box and free

all language from its ties no bonds repair no water
capture for its silhouettes I am the archaic through which
aching vowels compose nights in the needle of the eye
master switches ! reeds burning in the cannery of despair

bereave no more the loss of harmony the graces that
clung to trees though no leaf remains the grasses underfoot
lawns of Neolithic destiny its hills the fuming mysteries

all distances are One ! none is greater than the breath
that lingers above the mouth a year and many more a soul
linked to nothing but its other in name only a *sound*

FIN

Afterword

Three Hacks
by John M. Bennett

lake switch

words before cold the door
inches remnant of sleep
lacustrine syllables or some
thing wet his legs a grassy

shadow creaking in a labyrinth
of rivers comb your pants and
eyes writing breeze wrapped
in a mask's dense ants scarred

with dust with liquid words
bloody overleaf at the
fingers' origin tossed out the

entrance wet Intensive Care Unit's
gasping fish depronouncing a
red hieroglyph writhing in gravel

*Distortion of recombinant lines from
Iván Argüelles' Sonnets 39-40, 46-50*

language isn't this

as nervous then fail to notice shrinking
of sand in its tribulation to accumulate time
darkness around the swift of hair the swept
word a signal flashing in hidden decibels

last the inarticulate by you I have become
syntax of statues again becoming other than
ranunculus and butterfly thin streams of wind
will we too then pass through ears of sand

come back should you ever stair-top distance
and falling you detach shadow from frame
nor does anchored to clouds sleep resolve a

only to drown mirror face down in what were
dreamt or perhaps never been but in footnotes
none can read the remotely thumbed pages torn

*Recombinant shuffle of lines from
Iván Argüelles' Sonnets 1 - 8*

leaving the drugstore

the shadow its heat a tongue
brief letter E in lightless
grass blank toys and water
mark your buried knives

were heads shapeless ears a
rain map exhales yr book of
windows clocks wheels
sleeping inches from the wall

aphasia's wind speech
worms dancing in a body
box of burning alphabets

silhouettes spin in parentheses
doubled syntax missing your
marble doubt an inky flag dissolves

*Recombinant distorted condensation of
Iván Argüelles' Sonnets 92-100*

Other titles by Iván Argüelles
published by Luna Bisonte Prods:

LAGARTO DE MI CORAZÓN [2017]

FRAGMENTS FROM A GONE WORLD [2017]

LA INTERRUPCIÓN CONVERSACIONAL [2016]

ORPHIC CANTOS [2015]

DUO POEMATA:
ILION—A TRANSCRIPTION
& ALTERTUMSWISSENSCHAFT [2015]

FIAT LUX [2014]

A DAY IN THE SUN [2012]

ULTERIOR VISIONS [2011]

*Additional copies of this book
and of the above listed titles (mostly English language)
are available at:*

https://www.lulu.com/lunabisonteprods